Easy and  Noodles

Simple Noodle Cookbook for Quick Weekday Meals

By

Angel Burns

License Notices

This book or parts thereof might not be reproduced in any format for personal or commercial use without the written permission of the author. Possession and distribution of this book by any means without said permission is prohibited by law.

All content is for entertainment purposes and the author accepts no responsibility for any damages, commercially or personally, caused by following the content.

Table of Contents

Quick and Easy Noodle Recipes

HHHHHHHHHHHHHHHHHHHHHHHHHHHHHHHHHHHHHHHHHHH

Recipe 1: Hearty Beef Noodle Soup

This is the perfect noodle dish to serve whenever you are feeling under the weather. It will leave you feeling warm on the coldest night.

Yield: 6 servings

Preparation Time: 50 minutes

Ingredient List:

- 1 pound of beef stew meat, cut into small cubes
- 1 cup of onion, chopped
- 1 cup of celery, chopped
- ¼ cup of beef bouillon granules
- ¼ teaspoons of dried parsley
- Dash of black pepper
- 1 cup of carrots, chopped
- 5 ¾ cups of water
- 2 ½ cups of egg noodles, frozen

HHHHHHHHHHHHHHHHHHHHHHHHHHHHHHHHHHHHHHH

Instructions:

1. In a saucepan set over medium to high heat, add in the beef stew meat, chopped onion and chopped celery. Stir well to mix. Cook for 5 minutes or until the meat is browned.

2. Add in the beef bouillon granules, dash of black pepper, chopped carrots, water and frozen egg noodles. Stir well until evenly mixed.

3. Allow the mixture to come to a boil. Reduce the heat to low. Cook for 30 minutes.

4. Remove from heat and serve immediately.

Recipe 2: Easy Pad Thai

This is a delicious noodle dish you can make whenever you are craving a meal that is packed full of an exotic flavor.

Yield: 6 servings

Preparation Time: 1 hour

Ingredient List:

- 12 ounces of rice noodles, dried
- ½ cup of white sugar
- ½ cup of white vinegar, distilled
- ¼ cup of fish sauce
- 2 Tablespoons of tamarind paste
- 1 tablespoon of vegetable oil
- 2 chicken breasts, boneless, skinless and sliced into thin strips
- 1 tablespoon of vegetable oil
- 1 ½ teaspoons of garlic, minced
- 4 eggs, beaten
- 1 ½ Tablespoons of white sugar
- 1 ½ teaspoons of salt
- 1 cup of peanuts, ground
- 2 cups of bean sprouts
- ½ cup of chives, chopped
- 1 tablespoon of smoked paprika
- 1 lime, cut into wedges and for serving

HHHHHHHHHHHHHHHHHHHHHHHHHHHHHHHHHHHHHH

Instructions:

1. In a bowl, add in the rice noodles. Cover with water and set aside to soak for up to 1 hour. Drain and set aside.

2. In a saucepan placed over medium heat, add in the white sugar, vinegar, fish sauce and tamarind. Stir well to mix and bring to a simmer. Remove from heat and set aside.

3. In a skillet set over medium to high heat, add in 1 tablespoon vegetable oil. Add in the chicken and cook for 5 to 8 minutes or until cooked through. Remove from heat and set aside.

4. In a wok set over medium to high heat, add in 1 tablespoon vegetable oil. Add in the eggs. Cook for 1 to 2 minutes or until scrambled. Add in the cooked chicken and soaked noodles. Toss well to mix. Add in the tamarind, 1 ½ tablespoons of white sugar and dash of salt. Toss again to coat. Cook for 3 to 5 minutes or until the noodles are soft.

5. Add in the peanuts and continue to cook for an additional minute or until cooked through.

6. Remove from heat and serve with a garnish of the spouts, chives, paprika and lime wedges.

Recipe 3: Yakisoba Chicken

This is a classic and delicious Asian dish that you will love the moment you get a taste of it for yourself. One bite and you will never want to order from your local takeout restaurant ever again.

Yield: 6 servings

Preparation Time: 30 minutes

Ingredient List:

- ½ teaspoons of sesame oil
- 1 tablespoon of canola oil
- 2 Tablespoons of chile paste
- 2 cloves of garlic, chopped
- 4 chicken breasts, skinless, boneless and cut into small cubes
- ½ cup of soy sauce
- 1 onion, sliced thinly
- ½ of a head of cabbage, chopped
- 2 carrots, chopped
- 8 ounces of soba noodles, cooked

HHHHHHHHHHHHHHHHHHHHHHHHHHHHHHHHHHHHHHH

Instructions:

1. In a skillet set over medium heat, add in the sesame oil and chile paste. Cook for 30 seconds.

2. Add in the chopped garlic and continue to cook for another 30 seconds.

3. Add in the chicken cubes and ¼ cup of the soy sauce. Stir well until evenly mixed. Cook for 5 to 10 minutes or until browned. Transfer this mixture into a large bowl and set aside.

4. In the skillet, add in the chopped onion, chopped head of cabbage and chopped carrots. Stir well to mix and cook for 2 to 3 minutes or until the cabbage is wilted.

5. Add in the remaining ¼ cup of soy sauce, cooked soba noodles and the cooked chicken mixture. Toss well until evenly blended.

6. Remove from heat and serve immediately.

Recipe 4: Chicken Noodle Soup

This is a delicious and easy noodle soup you can make whenever you need something filling and savory dish to pick you up whenever you are feeling under the weather.

Yield: 12 servings

Preparation Time: 45 minutes

Ingredient List:

- 3 quarts of water
- 1, 32 ounce container of chicken stock
- 8 cubes of chicken bouillon
- 3 chicken breasts, skinless, boneless and cut into 1 inch pieces
- 4 egg noodles
- 1 cup of peas and carrots, mixed together
- 2 stalks of celery, chopped
- ¼ cup of onion, chopped
- 1 teaspoon of salt
- 1 teaspoon of black pepper
- ¼ teaspoons of dried basil
- 1/8 teaspoons of bay leaf, crushed
- 1/8 teaspoons of dried oregano

HHHHHHHHHHHHHHHHHHHHHHHHHHHHHHHHHHHHHH

[15]

Instructions:

1. In a large stock pot set over medium heat, add in the water, bouillon and chicken stock. Stir well to mix and bring to a boil.

2. Add in the chicken breast pieces, mixed peas and carrots, egg noodles, chopped celery, chopped onion, dried basil, crushed bay leaf and dried oregano. Season with a dash of salt and black pepper. Stir well to mix.

3. Boil for 20 minutes. Reduce the heat to medium. Continue to cook for 10 to 15 minutes or until the chicken is cooked.

Remove from heat and serve immediately.

Recipe 5: Healthy Cabbage and Noodles

This is a simple and delicious noodle dish that you can enjoy whenever you are craving something on the healthier side.

Yield: 4 servings

Preparation Time: 45 minutes

Ingredient List:

- 1, 8 ounce pack of egg noodles
- 3 Tablespoons of butter
- ½ pound of bacon
- 1 onion, chopped
- 1 head of cabbage, chopped
- Dash of garlic salt

HHHHHHHHHHHHHHHHHHHHHHHHHHHHHHHHHHHHHHHHHHH

Instructions:

1. Place a pot over medium heat. Fill with water and season with a dash of salt. Allow to come to a boil and add in the egg noodles. Cook for 8 to 10 minutes or until soft. Drain and place the egg noodles back into the pot. Add in the three tablespoons of butter and toss until coated. Set aside.

2. In a skillet set over medium to high heat, add in the bacon. Cook for 10 minutes or until crispy. Transfer onto a plate to drain.

3. In the same skillet with the bacon grease, add in the chopped onion. Cook for 5 minutes or until soft.

4. Add in the cabbage and cook for 5 minutes or until wilted.

5. Chop the bacon into small pieces and add back into the skillet. Toss to mix. Continue to cook for 10 minutes or until the cabbage is soft.

6. Remove from heat and serve immediately.

Recipe 6: Simple Hamburger Stroganoff

Just as the name implies, this is a delicious and simple dish you can make any night of the week. Smothered in a smooth sauce, this is a dish everybody will love it.

Yield: 6 servings

Preparation Time: 30 minutes

Ingredient List:

- 1, 16 ounce pack of egg noodles
- 1 pound of ground beef
- 1, .75 ounce pack of brown gravy mix
- 1, 8 ounce pack of cream cheese, soft
- 1, 6 ounce can of mushrooms, chopped
- ½ cup of whole milk
- 1, 8 ounce container of sour cream
- 2, 10.75 ounce cans of cream of mushroom soup, condensed

HHHHHHHHHHHHHHHHHHHHHHHHHHHHHHHHHHHHHH

Instructions:

1. Place a pot over high heat. Fill with water seasoned with salt. Allow to come to a boil. Add in the egg noodles and cook for 8 to 10 minutes or until soft. Drain and set aside.

2. In a skillet set over medium heat, add in the beef. Cook for 5 minutes or until no more pink shows in the meat. Drain the excess fat.

3. Add in the brown gravy mix, soft cream cheese and chopped mushrooms. Stir well to mix. Cook for 1 to 2 minutes or until the cheese melts completely.

4. Add in the whole milk, container of sour cream and can of mushroom soup. Stir well to mix.

5. Add in the cooked pasta and toss well to mix.

6. Remove from heat and serve immediately.

Recipe 7: Lazy Turkey Stroganoff

Just as the name implies, this is the perfect stroganoff dish for you to make whenever you are feeling particularly lazy. This is a creamy and delicious dish you can make with your leftover turkey from Thanksgiving.

Yield: 4 servings

Preparation Time: 35 minutes

Ingredient List:

- 1, 8 ounce pack of egg noodles
- 1 tablespoon of vegetable oil
- 1 pound of ground turkey
- 1 tablespoon of onion, minced
- 1 cube of chicken bouillon, crumbled
- 1, 10.75 ounce can of cream of mushroom soup, condensed
- ½ cup of water
- 1 tablespoon of smoked paprika
- Dash of salt

HHHHHHHHHHHHHHHHHHHHHHHHHHHHHHHHHHHHHHHHH

Instructions:

1. Place a pot over medium to high heat. Fill with water and season with a dash of salt. Allow to come to a boil. Add in the egg noodles. Cook for 10 minutes or until soft. Drain the egg noodles and set aside.

2. In a skillet set over medium heat, add in the tablespoon of vegetable oil. Add in the turkey and chopped onion. Stir well to mix. Cook for 8 to 10 minutes or until the meat is browned and the onion is soft.

3. Add in the crumbled chicken bouillon. Stir well to mix.

4. Add in the condensed cream of mushrooms soup and water. Stir well to mix.

5. Season with a tablespoon of smoked paprika and dash of salt. Stir well until evenly incorporated.

6. Sere the turkey mixture over the cooked egg noodles.

Recipe 8: Spicy Pork and Cabbage Stir Fry

This is a dish you can make whenever you have a need to have something with a bit of a kick to it. Stir fried to perfection, this is one dish you won't be able to resist.

Yield: 6 servings

Preparation Time: 45 minutes

Ingredient List:

- 12 ounces of Chinese noodles
- 3 Tablespoons of soy sauce
- ¾ cup of sweet chili sauce
- ½ teaspoons of powdered garlic
- ¼ teaspoons of ground ginger
- 3 Tablespoons of sesame oil
- ½ cup of soy sauce
- ½ teaspoons of powdered garlic
- 1, 1 pound of pork loin, cut into strips
- 2 Tablespoons of vegetable oil
- 2 onions, chopped
- 1/8 teaspoons of crushed red pepper flakes
- 3 Tablespoons of sweet chili sauce
- 3 cups of napa cabbage
- ¾ cup of celery, thinly sliced
- 3 red bell peppers, chopped
- 2 teaspoons of cornstarch
- ¼ cup of cold water

HHHHHHHHHHHHHHHHHHHHHHHHHHHHHHHHHHHHHHH

Instructions:

1. In a pot placed over medium heat, fill with water. Season with a dash of salt and allow to come to a boil. Add in the Chinese noodles. Cook for 5 minutes or until soft. Drain and set aside in a colander.

2. In a bowl, add in 3 tablespoons of the soy sauce, ¾ cup of the chili sauce, ½ teaspoon of powdered garlic, ground ginger and sesame oil. Whisk until evenly mixed. Add in the noodles and toss to coat.

3. In a separate bowl, add in ½ cup of the soy sauce and ½ teaspoons of the powdered garlic. Whisk to mix. Add in the pork and stir well to coat. Set aside to marinate for 5 minutes.

4. In a wok over medium to high heat, add in 1 to 2 tablespoons of vegetable oil. Add in the marinated pork, chopped onions and crushed red pepper flakes. Stir well to mix and cook for 5 minutes or until the pork is browned.

5. Add in 3 tablespoons of the chili sauce, cabbage, chopped celery, chopped carrots and chopped red bell peppers. Stir again to mix. Cook for 5 minutes or until soft.

6. In a small bowl, add in the cornstarch and water. Whisk until smooth in consistency. Pour into the wok and toss well to mix. Cook for 5 minutes or until thick in consistency.

7. Remove from heat. Serve the pork over the cooked noodles. Serve immediately.

Recipe 9: Korean Glass Noodles

This is a delicious appetizer this I know you won't be able to get enough of. It is a traditional dish that you can serve with a topping of chicken or beef.

Yield: 4 servings

Preparation Time: 20 minutes

Ingredient List:

- 1, 8 count pack of sweet potato vermicelli
- 12 cup of low sodium soy sauce
- ¼ cup of light brown sugar
- ½ cup of water, boiling
- 3 Tablespoons of vegetable oil
- 1 teaspoon of sesame seeds, toasted

HHHHHHHHHHHHHHHHHHHHHHHHHHHHHHHHHHHHH

Instructions:

1. Break the vermicelli in half and place into a large baking dish. Cover with hot water and set aside to soak for 10 minutes. Drain the noodles and set aside.

2. In a medium bowl, add in the low sodium soy sauce, light brown sugar and boiling water. Whisk until mixed and pour this mixture over the top of the drained noodles in a large bowl. Toss well to coat.

3. In a large skillet set over medium heat, add in the three tablespoons of vegetable oil. Add in the coated noodles and sauce mixture. Cook for 5 minutes.

4. Remove from heat and serve with a garnish of toasted sesame seeds.

Recipe 10: Turkey Tetrazzini

This is another hearty Italian dish I now you won't be able to get enough of. It is the perfect dish to make whenever you have leftover turkey.

Yield: 6 servings

Preparation Time: 45 minutes

Ingredient List:

- 1, 8 ounce pack of egg noodles, cooked
- 2 Tablespoons of butter, soft
- 1, 6 ounce can of mushrooms, thinly sliced
- 1 teaspoon of salt
- 1/8 teaspoons of black pepper
- 2 cups of turkey, cooked and chopped
- 1, 10.75 ounce can of cream of celery soup, condensed
- 1 cup of sour cream
- ½ cup of parmesan cheese, grated

HHHHHHHHHHHHHHHHHHHHHHHHHHHHHHHHHHHHHHH

Instructions:

1. Place a large pot over medium to high heat. Fill with water and allow to come to a boil. Season with a dash of salt and add in the egg noodles. Cook for 8 to 10 minutes or until soft. Drain and transfer into a large bowl. Set aside.

2. Preheat the oven to 375 degrees.

3. In a skillet set over medium heat, add in the two tablespoons of butter. Add in the sliced mushrooms and cook for 1 minute. Season with a dash of salt and black pepper.

4. Add in the cooked turkey, cream of celery soup and sour cream. Stir well to mix.

5. Add the drained egg noodles into a casserole dish. Pour the sauce over the top. Sprinkle the grated Parmesan cheese over the top.

6. Place into the oven to bake for 20 to 25 minutes.

7. Remove and cool for 5 minutes before serving.

Recipe 11: Asparagus and Chicken Casserole

This is a great tasting noodle dish for you to make whenever spring comes around. Be sure to use the freshest asparagus you can find.

Yield: 6 servings

Preparation Time: 1 hour and 15 minutes

Ingredient List:

- 1, 8 ounce pack of egg noodles
- 1 1/3 Tablespoons of extra virgin olive oil
- 1 onion, chopped
- 1 cup of chicken, cooked and chopped
- 1 red bell pepper, chopped
- 2 stalks of celery, chopped
- 1 cup of chicken stock
- 1 ½ cups of sour cream
- ½ teaspoons of dried oregano
- 1 pound of asparagus, trimmed and cut into small pieces
- 8 Tablespoons of Parmesan cheese, grated and evenly divided

HHHHHHHHHHHHHHHHHHHHHHHHHHHHHHHHHHHHHHH

Instructions:

1. Preheat the oven to 350 degrees. Grease a casserole dish.

2. In a pot over medium to high heat. Fill with water and season with salt. Add in the noodles and cook at a boil for 5 minutes or until soft. Drain the noodles and transfer into a large bowl.

3. In a skillet set over medium heat, add in the olive oil. Add in the onion and cook for 5 minutes or until soft.

4. Add in the chopped chicken, chopped red bell peppers, chopped celery and chicken stock. Stir well to mix. Bring the mixture to a boil and cook for 5 minutes.

5. Add in the sour cream and dried oregano. Stir well to incorporate.

6. Pour half of the chicken mixture into the casserole dish. Place the asparagus pieces over the top. Top off with the drained noodles. Add 5 tablespoons of parmesan cheese and top off with the remaining half of the chicken mixture. Sprinkle extra parmesan cheese over the top.

7. Place into the oven to bake for 30 minutes or until browned.

8. Remove and cool for 5 minutes before serving.

Recipe 12: Hungarian Pork Stew

This is a delicious dish to make whenever you are looking for a dish to impress your friends and family with something for any special occasion.

Yield: 14 servings

Preparation Time: 2 hours and 15 minutes

Ingredient List:

- 5 slices of bacon, chopped
- 2 onions, chopped
- ¼ cup of Hungarian paprika
- 1 ½ teaspoons of powdered garlic
- ¼ teaspoons of black pepper
- 5 pounds of pork chops, boneless
- 1 yellow bell pepper, seeds removed and chopped
- 2, 14 ounce cans of tomatoes, chopped
- 2/3 cup of beef broth
- 2 cups of low fat sour cream
- 2, 6 ounce packs of egg noodles

HHHHHHHHHHHHHHHHHHHHHHHHHHHHHHHHHHHHHH

Instructions:

1. In a skillet set over medium to high heat, add in the bacon. Cook for 10 minutes or until browned. Transfer the bacon onto a large plate and drain all but 1 tablespoon of bacon grease.

2. In the same skillet, add in the chopped onions. Cook for 5 minutes or until soft. Remove the skillet from heat. Add in the Hungarian paprika, powdered garlic and dash of black pepper. Stir well to mix and transfer into a stockpot.

3. In a small skillet, add in 1 tablespoon of the bacon drippings. Add in the pork chops and cook for 5 minutes on both sides or until browned. Remove and place the chops onto a large plate. Blot dry with a few paper towels. Chop into small pieces.

4. In the same small skillet, add in the yellow bell pepper pieces. Cook for 5 minutes or until soft. Remove and transfer the peppers into the bacon mixture. Stir well to mix.

5. In a stockpot set over medium to high heat, add in the cans of tomatoes along with the liquid from the cans and beef broth. Stir well to mix. Bring this mixture to a simmer.

6. Add in the bacon and pepper mixture into the stockpot. Stir well to incorporate. Cook for 90 minutes or until the mixture is thick in consistency.

7. In a pot set over medium heat. Fill with water and season with a dash of salt. Add in the egg noodles and cook for 5 minutes or until soft. Drain the noodles and place onto serving plate.

8. Add the sour cream into the stew and stir well until incorporate. Spoon the beef stew over the noodles and serve immediately.

Recipe 13: Udon Peanut Butter Noodles

This is a delicious Thai dish you can make whenever you are craving something on the exotic side. It contains a spicy kick that I know you will find irresistible.

Yield: 6 servings

Preparation Time: 45 minutes

Ingredient List:

- 1, 9 ounce pack of udon noodles, dried
- ½ cup of chicken broth
- 1 ½ Tablespoons of ginger, minced
- 3 Tablespoons of soy sauce
- 3 Tablespoons of peanut butter, smooth
- 1 ½ Tablespoons of honey
- 2 teaspoons of chili oil
- 3 cloves of garlic, minced
- 1 rotisserie chicken, meat shredded
- 1 red bell pepper, sliced
- ¼ cup of green onions, chopped
- ¼ cup of peanuts, chopped
- ¼ cup of cilantro, chopped

HHHHHHHHHHHHHHHHHHHHHHHHHHHHHHHHHHHHH

Instructions:

1. Place a large pot over medium heat. Fill with salted water and bring to a boil. Add in the udon noodles and boil for 10 to 12 minutes or until soft. Drain the noodles and set aside in a large bowl.

2. In a medium saucepan set over medium to high heat, add in the chicken broth, minced ginger, soy sauce, smooth peanut butter, honey, oil and minced garlic. Whisk until evenly mixed.

3. Bring the sauce to a boil and cook for 3 minutes or until the peanut butter is melted. Remove from heat and pour over the udon noodles. Toss to coat.

4. Add in the shredded chicken and sliced red bell pepper. Toss well to mix.

5. Serve immediately with a sprinkling of green onions, peanuts and chopped cilantro.

Recipe 14: Meatballs and Buttered Meatballs

This is the perfect noodle dish for you to make whenever you are craving homemade Italian food. It is so tasty, even the pickiest of children will be begging for seconds.

Yield: 24 servings

Preparation Time: 3 hours and 15 minutes

Ingredient List:

- 2, 10.75 ounce can of cream of celery soup, condensed
- 2, 10.5 ounce can of French onion soup, condensed
- 1, 16 ounce container of sour cream
- 6 pounds of Italian meatballs
- 2, 16 ounce packs of egg noodles
- ½ cup of butter, soft

HHHHHHHHHHHHHHHHHHHHHHHHHHHHHHHHHHHHHHH

Instructions:

1. In a slow cooker, add in the cream of celery and French onion soup. Add in the container of sour cream and meatballs. Stir well until evenly mixed.

2. Cover and cook on the highest setting for 3 to 4 hours.

3. In a pot set over medium to high heat, add in water. Season with a dash of salt and allow to come to a boil. Add in the egg noodles. Cook for 8 to 10 minutes or until soft. Drain and transfer into a large bowl.

4. In the bowl, add in the soft butter. Toss until coated.

5. Serve the meatballs on top of a bed of the buttered noodles.

Recipe 15: Vietnamese Rice Noodle Salad

This is a delicious dish you can make whenever you are craving something on the healthier and light side. It is perfect for you to make during the hot summer months.

Yield: 4 servings

Preparation Time: 15 minutes

Ingredient List:

- 5 cloves of garlic, minced
- 1 cup of cilantro, chopped
- ½ of a jalapeno pepper, seeds removed and minced
- 3 Tablespoons of white sugar
- ¼ cup of lime juice
- 3 Tablespoons of vegetarian friendly fish sauce
- 1, 12 ounce of dried rice noodles
- 2 carrots, cut julienne style
- 1 cucumber, cut into halves and chopped
- ¼ cup of mint, chopped
- 4 leaves of napa cabbage
- ¼ cup of peanuts, chopped
- 4 sprigs of mint, chopped

HHHHHHHHHHHHHHHHHHHHHHHHHHHHHHHHHHHHHHHH

Instructions:

1. In a large bowl, add in the minced garlic, chopped cilantro, fresh lime juice, vegetarian fish sauce, white sugar and minced jalapeno pepper. Stir well to mix. Set aside to rest for 5 minutes.

2. In a large pot set of medium heat, fill with salted water. Bring to a boil. Add in the rice noodles and boil for 2 minutes or until soft. Drain the noodles and set into a large bowl.

3. In the same bowl, add in the sauce, chopped carrots, chopped cucumber, chopped mint leaves and cabbage. Toss well to coat.

4. Serve immediately with a garnish of chopped peanuts and chopped mint.

Recipe 16: Hamburger Casserole

Make this delicious noodle dish whenever you need to get dinner ready for your family in a hurry. It is so tasty; your entire family will be begging you to make this as often as possible.

Yield: 6 servings

Preparation Time: 40 minutes

Ingredient List:

- 1 pound of ground beef
- 1 onion, chopped
- 1 stalk of celery, chopped
- 8 ounces of egg noodles
- 1, 15 ounce can of chili
- 1, 14.5 ounce can of tomatoes, peeled and chopped
- 1, 15 ounce can of whole kernel corn, drained
- ¼ cup of mild salsa
- 1, 1 ounce pack of taco seasoning mix

HHHHHHHHHHHHHHHHHHHHHHHHHHHHHHHHHHHH

Instructions:

1. Preheat the oven to 250 degrees.

2. In a skillet set over medium heat, add in the ground beef, chopped onion and chopped celery. Stir well to mix and cook for 10 minutes or until the beef is browned. Drain the excess grease and set aside.

3. In a saucepan set over medium heat, prepare the noodles according to the directions on the package. Drain the noodles and place the noodles back into the saucepan.

4. Add in the beef and onion mixture, mild chili, chopped tomatoes, can of corn and taco seasoning mix. Toss well until evenly mixed.

5. Spread the mixture into a casserole dish.

6. Place into the oven to bake for 20 minutes. Remove and cool for 5 minutes before serving.

Recipe 17: Pasta Primavera

This is another noodle dish that every Italian food lover in your home will fall in love with. It is an easy and delicious dish to make whenever you need to get your daily dose of vegetables.

Yield: 8 servings

Preparation Time: 50 minutes

Ingredient List:

- 1, 16 ounce pack of whole wheat penne pasta
- 2 Tablespoons of extra virgin olive oil
- 2 zucchinis, chopped
- 1 green bell pepper, chopped
- 2 carrots, chopped
- 1, 8 ounce pack of mushrooms, thinly sliced
- 3 onions, chopped
- 3 cloves of garlic, minced
- 1, 14.5 ounce can of tomatoes, stewed and chopped
- 1 cup of low sodium chicken broth
- 2 Tablespoons of parsley, chopped
- ½ teaspoons of dried basil
- ½ teaspoons of dried oregano
- ½ teaspoons of crushed red pepper flakes
- 2 Tablespoons of grated Parmesan cheese
- 2/3 cup of smoked Gouda cheese, shredded

HHHHHHHHHHHHHHHHHHHHHHHHHHHHHHHHHHHHHHH

Instructions:

1. Place a pot over medium to high heat. Fill with water. Add in the penne pasta and allow to boil for 11 to 12 minutes or until soft. Drain the pasta and place into a large bowl. Set aside.

2. In a skillet set over medium heat, add in the olive oil. Add in the chopped zucchini, chopped green bell pepper, chopped carrots, sliced mushrooms and chopped onion. Stir well until evenly mixed. Cook for 5 to 10 minutes or until soft.

3. Add in the garlic and cook for an additional minute.

4. Add in the can of tomatoes, chicken broth, chopped parsley, dried basil, crushed red pepper flakes and dried oregano. Stir until evenly incorporated.

5. Bring to mixture to a boil. Reduce the heat to low and cook for 5 minutes or until the sauce is thick in consistency.

6. Add in the cooked penne pasta and toss well to mix. Cook for 2 minutes.

7. Remove from heat. Top off with the grated Parmesan cheese and shredded Gouda cheese.

8. Serve immediately.

Recipe 18: Classic Chinese Fried Noodles

Whenever you are craving authentic Chinese food, then this is one dish you will want to make. It is incredibly easy to make, you will be able to put it together in no time at all.

Yield: 6 servings

Preparation Time: 40 minutes

Ingredient List:

- 2, 3 ounce pack of ramen noodles, oriental flavored
- 3 eggs, beaten
- Vegetable oil, as needed
- 4 green onions, thinly sliced
- 1 carrot, peeled and grated
- ½ cup of green peas
- ¼ cup of red bell pepper, minced
- 2 Tablespoons of sesame oil
- Soy sauce, as needed

HHHHHHHHHHHHHHHHHHHHHHHHHHHHHHHHHHHHHH

Instructions:

1. In a saucepan set over medium heat, fill with water. Allow to come to a boil and add in the ramen noodles. Cook for 5 minutes or until soft. Set the flavor packets aside and drain the noodles. Set the noodles into a large bowl and set aside.

2. In a skillet set over medium heat, add in 1 tablespoon vegetable oil.

3. In a small bowl, add in the eggs and whisk until beaten lightly. Pour the beaten eggs into the skillet and cook for 2 minutes or until set. Remove the eggs and set aside.

4. In a separate skillet, add in a teaspoon of the vegetable oil. Add in the green onions. Cook for 3 minutes or until soft. Transfer onto a small plate and set aside.

5. Add another teaspoon vegetable oil in the same skillet. Add in the grated carrots, green peas and minced bell pepper. Stir well to mix and cook for 5 minutes or until soft. Remove and transfer onto a small plate. Set aside.

6. Set a large wok over medium heat. Add in 2 tablespoons of sesame and 1 tablespoon vegetable oil. Add in the ramen noodles. Toss well to mix and cook for 5 minutes or until soft. Add in the soy sauce, sesame oil and ramen seasoning. Toss to coat.

7. Add in the cooked vegetable and toss to coat. Continue to cook for 5 minutes.

8. Remove from heat and serve immediately.

Recipe 19: Afghan Beef Raviolis

While this dish may take some time to prepare, it is well worth the effort in the end. It is so delicious, you will swear it came from a five star restaurant.

Yield: 4 servings

Preparation Time: 2 hours and 10 minutes

Ingredient List:

- ¾ cup of plain Greek yogurt
- 1 teaspoon of mint leaves, chopped
- 2 cloves of garlic, crushed
- 1 pound of lean ground beef
- 1 ½ cups of onion, chopped
- 1 cup of water
- 1 carrot, grated
- ¾ teaspoons of salt
- 1 teaspoon of black pepper
- 1 ½ teaspoons of ground coriander
- ½ teaspoons of ground cumin
- 26 wonton wrappers
- 1 tablespoon of tomato paste
- 1/8 teaspoons of crushed red pepper flakes
- 2 Tablespoons of water
- ½ cup of yellow split peas
- 1/8 teaspoons of crushed red pepper flakes
- 1 teaspoon of ground coriander
- ¼ teaspoons of ground cumin
- 1 cube of chicken bouillon
- 1 ½ cups of water

Instructions:

1. In a small bowl, add in the plain yogurt, chopped mint leaves and crushed garlic. Stir well to mix and set aside in the fridge to chill.

2. In a large skillet set over medium heat, add in the beef and chopped onions. Cook for 8 to 10 minutes or until the beef is browned. Drain the excess grease.

3. Add in 1 cup of water, chopped carrot, the ground cumin, ground coriander and a dash of salt and black pepper. Stir well to mix. Cook for 30 minutes or until all of the water has evaporated.

4. Place the wonton wrappers onto a sheet of aluminum foil. Add 2 tablespoons of the beef into the center of each wrapper. Fold over the filling and press the edges. Repeat with the remaining wrappers and filling.

5. Transfer into a streamer. Steam for 40 minutes.

6. In a large bowl, add in the yellow split peas, 1/8 crushed red pepper flakes, teaspoon of coriander, ¼ teaspoon of cumin, bouillon and 1 ½ cups of water. Stir well to mix. Bring the mixture to a boil and reduce the heat to low. Cook for 45 minutes or until thick in consistency.

7. In a large skillet, add in the remaining meat mixture, 2 tablespoons of water, tomato paste and 1/8 teaspoon of crushed red pepper flakes. Stir well to mix and cook over low heat for 10 minutes.

8. Spread the yogurt onto a large plate. Place the ravioli and split pea mixture over the top. Top off with the remaining beef and tomato mixture. Serve immediately.

Recipe 20: Beef Stroganoff

This is yet another noodle dish I know you won't be able to get enough of. It is so delicious, I guarantee it will be a hit in your home.

Yield: 8 servings

Preparation Time: 30 minutes

Ingredient List:

- 1, 12 ounce pack of egg noodles, cooked
- 6 ounces of mushrooms, thinly sliced
- 1 onion, chopped
- ¼ cup of butter, soft
- 2 pounds of ground beef
- 4 Tablespoons of all-purpose flour
- 2 cups of beef broth
- 1 cup of sour cream
- Dash of salt and black pepper

HHHHHHHHHHHHHHHHHHHHHHHHHHHHHHHHHHHHH

Instructions:

1. Place a pot over medium heat. Fill with water and allow to come to a boil. Add in the noodles and cook for 10 minutes or until soft. Then drain the noodles and set aside.

2. In a skillet set over medium heat, add in the sliced mushrooms and chopped onions. Stir well to mix. Add in 2 tablespoons of butter. Cook for 5 to 8 minutes or until soft. Remove the mixture and transfer into a medium bowl. Set the mixture aside.

3. In the same skillet, add in the remaining butter and the ground beef. Cook for 8 to 10 minutes or until browned.

4. Add in the white flour, beef broth and mushroom mixture. Stir well to mix and cook for 5 minutes or until thick in consistency.

5. Add in the sour cream and stir well to incorporate.

6. Season with a dash of salt and black pepper. Remove from heat.

7. Serve immediately over the cooked egg noodles.

Recipe 21: Easy Tuna and Noodle Casserole

This is the perfect dish to serve whenever you need a filling dish to serve to serve a large group of people. It is so delicious, even the pickiest of eaters won't be able to resist this dish for long.

Yield: 6 servings

Preparation Time: 35 minutes

Ingredient List:

- 1, 12 ounce pack of egg noodles
- ¼ cup of onion, chopped
- 2 cups of cheddar cheese, shredded
- 1 cup of green peas, frozen
- 2, 5 ounce cans of tuna
- 2, 10.75 ounce cans of cream of mushroom soup, condensed
- ½, 4.5 ounce can of mushrooms, thinly sliced
- 1 cup of potato chips, crushed

HHHHHHHHHHHHHHHHHHHHHHHHHHHHHHHHHHHHHHHHHH

Instructions:

1. Place a large pot over medium heat. Fill with salted water and bring the water to a boil. Add in the egg noodles. Cook for 8 to 10 minutes or until soft. Drain the pasta and set aside.

2. Preheat the oven to 425 degrees.

3. In a large bowl, add in the cooked noodles, chopped onion, 1 cup of the shredded cheddar cheese, frozen green peas, cans of drained tuna, cream of mushrooms soup and sliced mushrooms Stir well to mix.

4. Transfer this mixture into a large baking dish.

5. Top off with the crushed potato chips and remaining cup of shredded cheese.

6. Place into the oven to bake for 15 to 20 minutes.

7. Remove and cool for 5 minutes before serving.

Recipe 22: Beef Tips with Noodles

This is another delicious and easy dish you can make whenever you need something convenient to prepare for your family. Best of all, it only uses a few ingredients, making it perfect for those who are on a strict budget.

Yield: 8 servings

Preparation Time: 1 hour and 15 minutes

Ingredient List:

- 1 pound of sirloin tips, cut into cubes
- 1, 10.75 ounce can of cream of mushroom soup, condensed
- 1, 1.25 ounce pack of beef and onion soup mix
- 1, 4.5 ounce can of mushrooms, chopped and drained
- 1 cup of water
- 1, 16 ounce pack of egg noodles, wide

HHHHHHHHHHHHHHHHHHHHHHHHHHHHHHHHHHHHHH

Instructions:

1. Preheat the oven to 400 degrees.

2. In a large casserole dish, add in the chopped mushrooms, can of mushroom soup, been and onion soup mix and water. Stir well until evenly mixed.

3. Add in the beef cubes and stir well to mix.

4. Place into the oven to bake for 1 hour.

5. In a pot set over high heat, add in water seasoned with salt. Bring the water to a boil. Add in the egg noodles and cook for 10 minutes or until soft. Drain and place the noodles onto serving plates.

6. Top off with the beef mixture and serve immediately.

Recipe 23: Pizza Casserole

If you love the taste of pizza, then this is the perfect dish for you to make. Feel free to top this casserole off with your favorite pizza toppings for the tastiest results.

Yield: 7 servings

Preparation Time: 1 hour

Ingredient List:

- 2 cups of egg noodles, uncooked
- ½ pound of ground beef
- 1 onion, chopped
- 2 cloves of garlic, minced
- 1 green bell pepper, sliced
- 1 cup of pepperoni sausage, thinly sliced
- 16 ounces of pizza sauce
- 4 Tablespoons of whole milk
- 1 cup of mozzarella cheese, shredded

HHHHHHHHHHHHHHHHHHHHHHHHHHHHHHHHHHHHHH

Instructions:

1. Prepare the egg noodles according to the directions on the package.

2. Preheat the oven to 350 degrees.

3. In a medium skillet set over medium to high heat, add in the lean ground beef, chopped onion, minced garlic and chopped bell pepper. Stir well to mix. Cook for 8 to 10 minutes or until the beef is cooked through. Drain the excess grease.

4. Add in the cooked egg noodles, sliced pepperoni, pizza sauce and whole milk. Stir well to mix.

5. Pour the mixture into a casserole dish.

6. Place into the oven to bake for 20 minutes.

7. Add the shredded mozzarella cheese over the top. Place back into the oven to bake for 5 to 10 minutes.

8. Remove and serve immediately.

Recipe 24: Cheesy Smothered Ramen Noodles

This is the perfect dish for you to make whenever you need something on the cheap side to make. Made with only a handful of ingredients, this is a dish that won't break the ban in the process.

Yield: 1 serving

Preparation Time: 5 minutes

Ingredient List:

- 2 cups of water
- 1, 3 ounce pack of ramen noodles, any flavor
- 1 slice of American cheese

HHHHHHHHHHHHHHHHHHHHHHHHHHHHHHHHHHHHHHHH

Instructions:

1. In a medium saucepan set over medium heat, fill with water. Allow the water to come to a boil.

2. Add the ramen noodles into the saucepan and cook for 4 minutes or until soft. Drain and place the noodles back into the saucepan.

3. Add in the seasoning packet and slice of American cheese. Toss well until the cheese is melted.

4. Remove from heat and serve immediately.

Recipe 25: Amish Casserole

This is a sweet and savory dish that is straight from the homes of the Amish from Pennsylvania Dutch country. One bite and I know you will want to make it for dinner nearly every night.

Yield: 6 servings

Preparation Time: 55 minutes

Ingredient List:

- 1 pound of lean ground beef
- 1, 10.75 ounce can of tomato soup, condensed
- ¼ cup of light brown sugar
- 1/8 teaspoons of black pepper
- ¼ teaspoons of salt
- 1, 10.75 ounce can of cream of chicken soup
- 1, 12 ounce pack of egg noodles
- 10 slices of American cheese

HHHHHHHHHHHHHHHHHHHHHHHHHHHHHHHHHHHHHH

Instructions:

1. Preheat the oven to 350 degrees.

2. Place a pot over medium heat and fill with water. Season with a dash of salt. Allow to come to a boil and add in the egg noodles. Cook for 8 to 10 minutes or until soft. Drain the egg noodles and place back into the pot.

3. Add in the chicken soup into the pot with the noodles. Toss until coated. Set aside.

4. In a skillet set over medium to high heat, add in the ground beef. Cook for 8 to 10 minutes or until browned. Drain the excess grease.

5. In the skillet, add I the tomato soup, light brown sugar, dash of salt and dash of black pepper. Stir well until evenly mixed. Remove from heat.

6. Spread the beef mixture into the bottom of a casserole dish. Place 5 slices of American cheese over the top of the beef. Add half of the noodles over the cheese and repeat the layers one more time, ending with the slices of cheese over the top.

7. Place into the oven to bake for 35 minutes.

8. Remove and cool for 5 minutes before serving.

About the Author

Angel Burns learned to cook when she worked in the local seafood restaurant near her home in Hyannis Port in Massachusetts as a teenager. The head chef took Angel under his wing and taught the young woman the tricks of the trade for cooking seafood. The skills she had learned at a young age helped her get accepted into Boston University's Culinary Program where she also minored in business administration.

Summers off from school meant working at the same restaurant but when Angel's mentor and friend retired as head chef, she took over after graduation and created classic and new dishes that delighted the diners. The restaurant flourished under Angel's culinary creativity and one customer developed more than an appreciation for Angel's food. Several months after taking over the position, the young woman met her future husband at work and they have been inseparable ever since. They still live in Hyannis Port with their two children and a cocker spaniel named Buddy.

Angel Burns turned her passion for cooking and her business acumen into a thriving e-book business. She has authored several successful books on cooking different types of dishes using simple ingredients for novices and experienced chefs alike. She is still head chef in Hyannis Port and says she will probably never leave!

Author's Afterthoughts

With so many books out there to choose from, I want to thank you for choosing this one and taking precious time out of your life to buy and read my work. Readers like you are the reason I take such passion in creating these books.

It is with gratitude and humility that I express how honored I am to become a part of your life and I hope that you take the same pleasure in reading this book as I did in writing it.

Can I ask one small favour? I ask that you write an honest and open review on Amazon of what you thought of the book. This will help other readers make an informed choice on whether to buy this book.

My sincerest thanks,

Angel Burns

If you want to be the first to know about news, new books, events and giveaways, subscribe to my newsletter by clicking the link below

https://angel-burns.gr8.com

or Scan QR-code

Printed in Great Britain
by Amazon